The ABCs

OF

BLACK INVENTORS

Published in the United States by
Beckham Publications Group, Inc.
PO Box 4066, Silver Spring, MD 20914

ISBN: 978-0-9823876-2-7
0-9823876-2-8
LCCN: 2009922872

For Dana –

Open Your Mind, and Invent Your Future

Also by Craig Thompson:

The ABCs of Black History: A Children's Guide

The ABCs

OF

BLACK INVENTORS

A Children's Guide

By Craig Thompson   Illustrated by Roger James

A Thompson Communications Book

Beckham Publications Group, Inc.
PO Box 4066, Silver Spring, MD 20914

Listen and learn, every boy and girl,
what black inventors have shared with the world

Aa

Andrew Beard made
connecting trains easy
The Jenny Coupler used
big hooks that were greasy

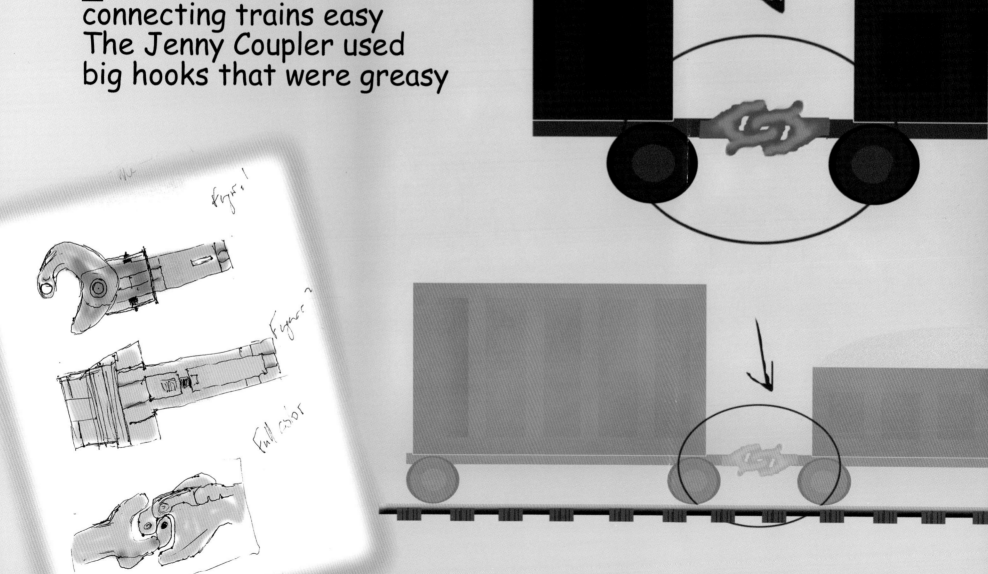

Bb

Bessie Blount practiced
science with heart
Her invention helped
soldiers to get a fresh start

Cc

Charles Drew's work
should make us give thanks
His knowledge and research
created blood banks

Dd

Donald Cotton should
be mentioned, of course
He travelled the world
for an energy source

Ff

Folding beds can
be slept on daily
Thanks to the work
of L.C. Bailey

Gg

Granville Woods made
the telegraph plain
So railroad conductors
could talk train to train

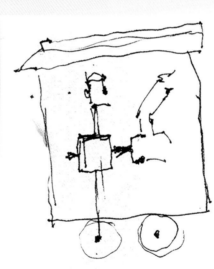

Hh

Henry Blair helped
Farmers meet their needs
By inventing a machine
for planting seeds

Ii

Ice cream is a treat
that everyone savors
Because Augustus Jackson
invented so many flavors

Jj

Jane Cooke Wright studied
treatments for cancer
She researched for years
to find an answer

Kk

Kevin Woolfolk liked to
watch animals run
His workout wheel lets
hamsters have fun

Ll

Lewis Latimer improved
the electric light
And now we see clearly,
even at night

Mm

Madame CJ Walker made
many women smile
Her products allowed
them to comb hair with style

Madam-CJ Walker
Hair Dress

Hair Dress

Madam-CJ Walker

Make-Up

Nn

Newman Marshman did
not seek any hype
With Lee Burridge he
built a machine used to type

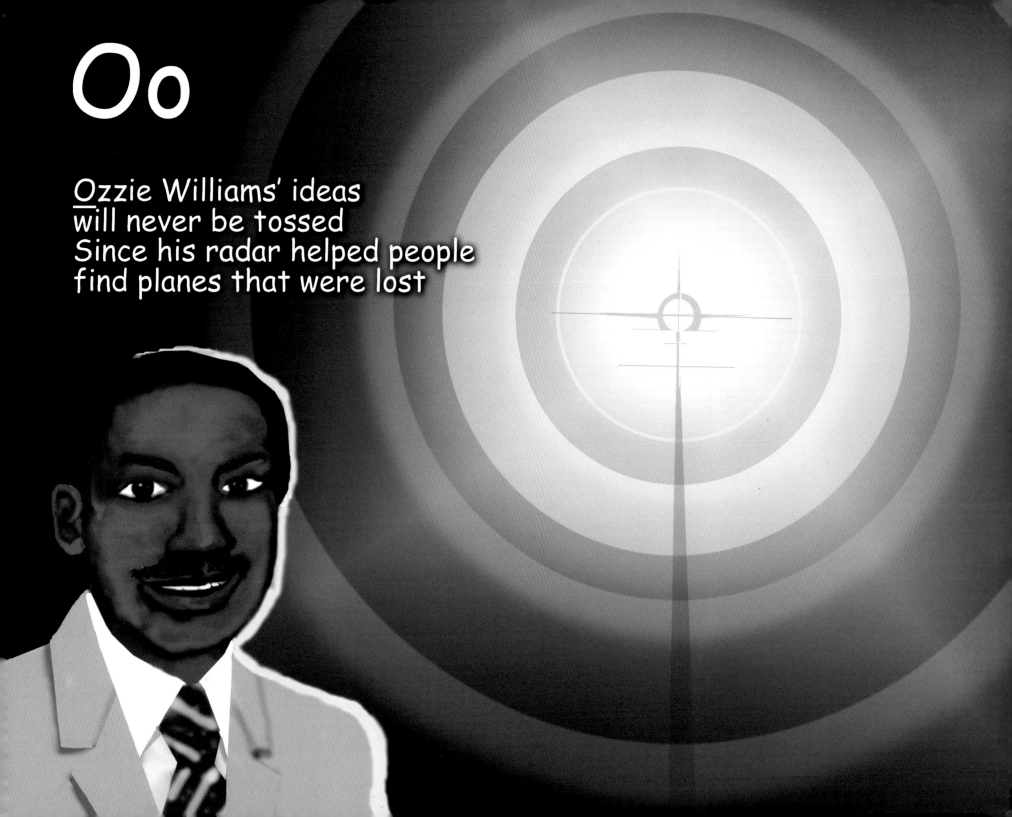

Oo

Ozzie Williams' ideas
will never be tossed
Since his radar helped people
find planes that were lost

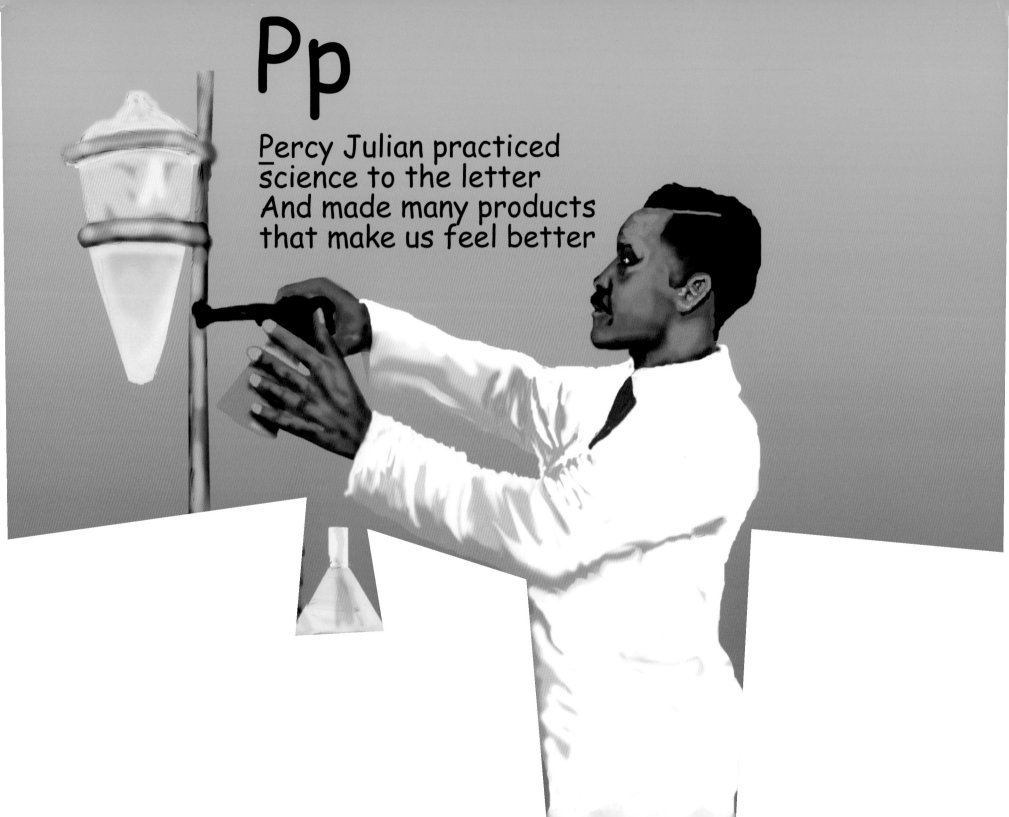

Pp

Percy Julian practiced
science to the letter
And made many products
that make us feel better

Qq

Quilting frames
had many uses
Because Thomas Elkins
made no excuses

Rr

Robert Allen helped us
track nickels and dimes
His coin counting tube
came right on time

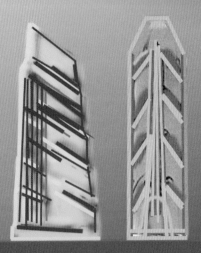

Ss

Sarah Boone loved style
and it certainly shows
Because of her we can
iron our clothes

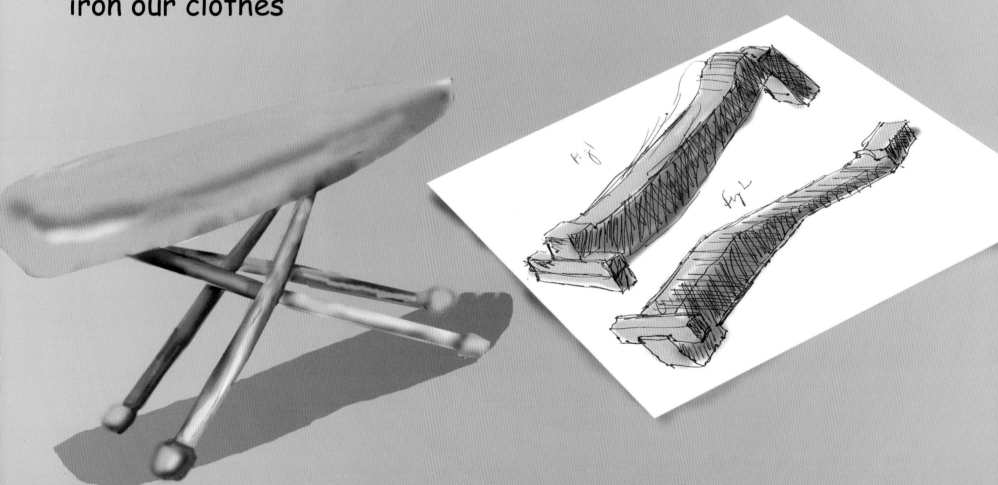

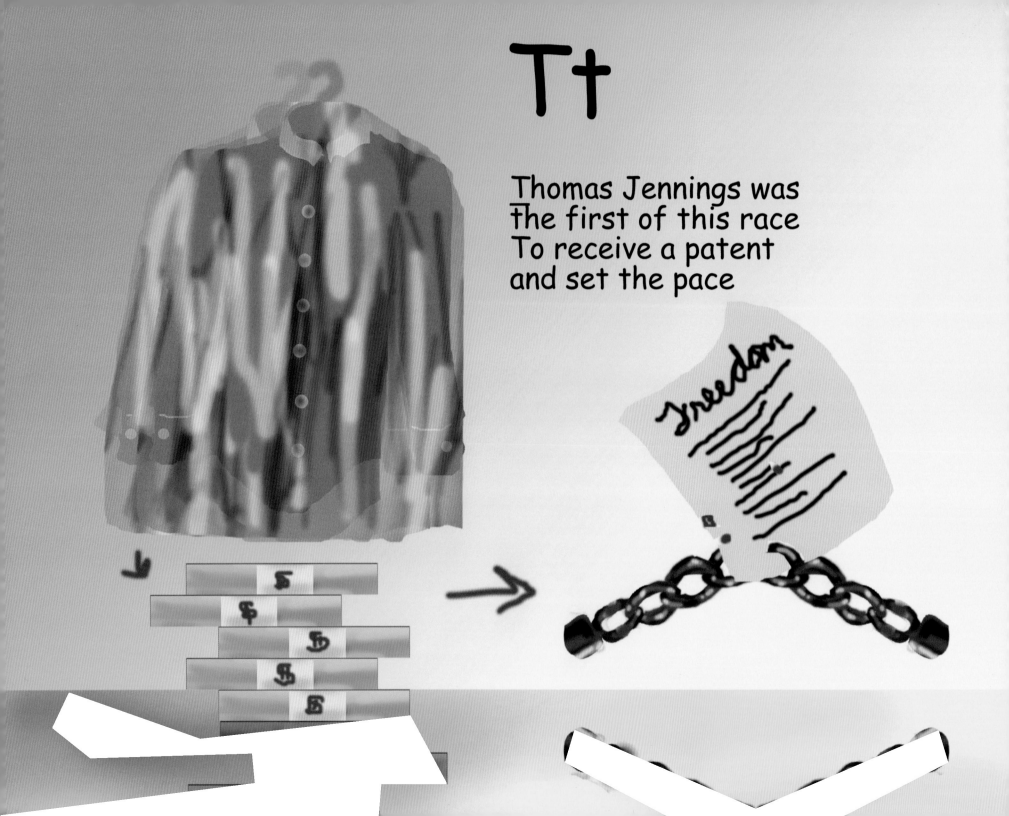

Tt

Thomas Jennings was
The first of this race
To receive a patent
and set the pace

Uu

Ultraviolet Cameras are
proving their worth
Since George Carruthers
found ways to look at the Earth

Vv

Virgil Trice's deeds
stand tall like a tower
He spent many years
studying nuclear power

Ww

William Purvis wanted us
to write clearly
His fountain pen helps,
and we thank him dearly

Xx

X-Ray Machines could be
moved space to space
Because Frederick Jones
had a vision in place

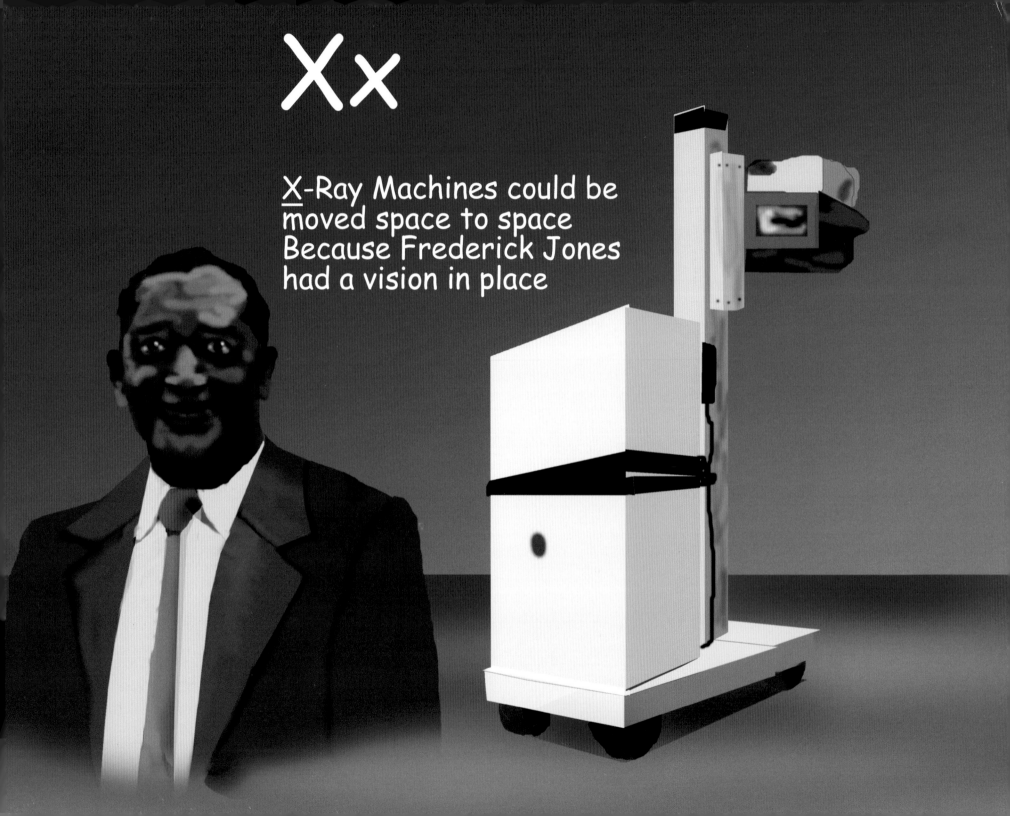

n can get tangled
and bend like a folder
So Julia Hammonds
designed a yarn holder

Zz

Zirconia became a
beautiful sight
When Jonathan Smith
made it nice and bright